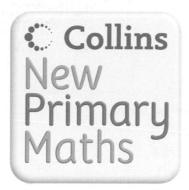

Collins New Primary Maths

Pupil Book 3B

Series Editor: Peter Clarke

Authors: Jeanette Mumford, Sandra Roberts, Andrew Edmondson

Contents

Sweet estimating

● **Estimate up to about 100 objects**

Work in pairs.

Take turns to point out a sweets pattern to your partner. Ask your partner to guess the number of sweets. Now count the actual number of sweets. Find the best way to guess.

The number on the label shows how many sweets are in a full jar. Estimate how many sweets are in each jar.

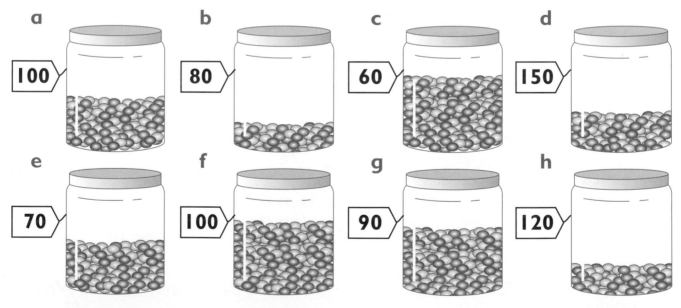

a 100 b 80 c 60 d 150

e 70 f 100 g 90 h 120

A game for 2 or 3 players.
● Take it in turns to pick up a handful of cubes and drop them on the sheet of paper.
● Each player then estimates the number of cubes on the paper.
● Count the cubes.
● The player with the closest estimate wins one point.

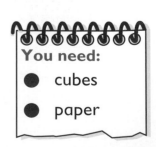

You need:
● cubes
● paper

Rabbit rounding up

● **Round any two-digit number to the nearest 10**

How far has each rabbit travelled? Write your answer to the nearest 10 metres.

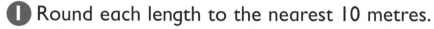

30   40   50   metres

1 Round each length to the nearest 10 metres.

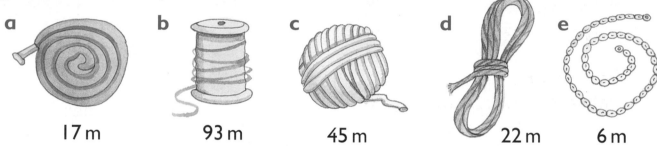

a 17 m   b 93 m   c 45 m   d 22 m   e 6 m

2 Round each distance to the nearest 10 metres.

a Beach 35 m   b Park 53 m   c Library 18 m   d Museum 96 m   e Toilets 104 m

The lengths of the fish have been rounded to the nearest 10 cm. Write five possible lengths for each fish.

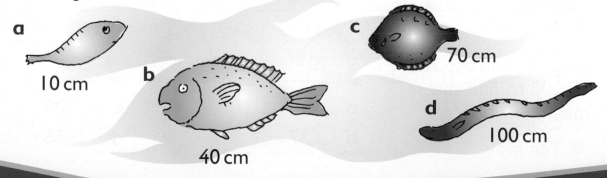

a 10 cm   b 40 cm   c 70 cm   d 100 cm

Firefighter number patterns

Explain how the digits in a number change when counting in 10s or 100s

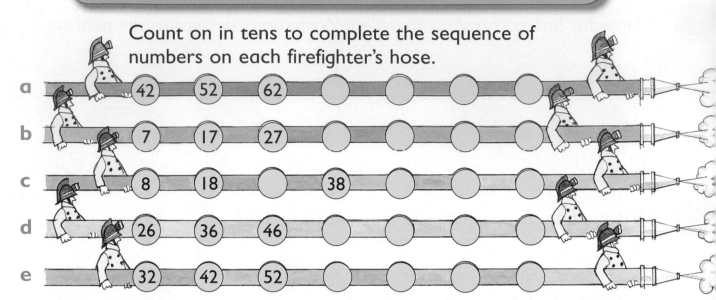

Count on in tens to complete the sequence of numbers on each firefighter's hose.

a 42 52 62 ○ ○ ○ ○

b 7 17 27 ○ ○ ○ ○

c 8 18 ○ 38 ○ ○ ○

d 26 36 46 ○ ○ ○ ○

e 32 42 52 ○ ○ ○ ○

Help the firefighters up or down the ladder by adding or subtracting 10 or 100 each time to or from the number on their coats.

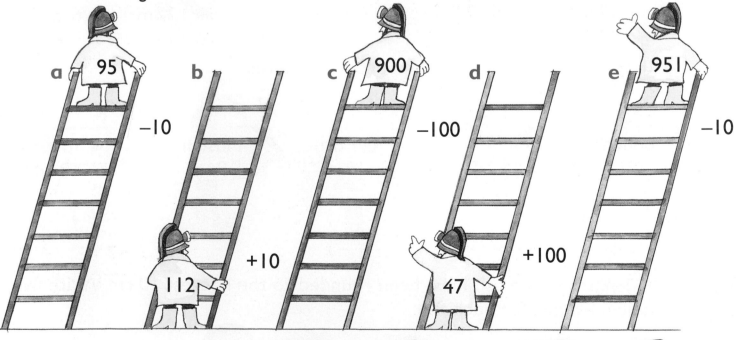

a 95   b   −10   112   c 900   −100   d   +100   47   e 951   −10   +10

Add or subtract 20 or 200 to find the missing numbers.

 −20 +20   −200 +200

a ☐ 20 ☐ ☐ ☐   c ☐ 300 ☐ ☐ ☐

b ☐ 37 ☐ ☐ ☐   d ☐ 475 ☐ ☐ ☐

Racing calculations

● **Add or subtract pairs of two-digit numbers**

 1 Work out the calculations using the steps in the boxes to help you.

 **2** Work out these calculations. Remember to add or subtract the tens first, then the units.

a 14 + 13

14 +10= ☐
☐ + 3 = ☐
14 +13= ☐

b 14 – 13

14 –10= ☐
☐ – 3 = ☐
14 –13= ☐

16 12   25 13   26 14   20 12   17 11

a 16 + 12
16 – 12

b 25 + 13
25 – 13

c 26 + 14
26 – 14

d 20 + 12
20 – 12

e 17 + 11
17 – 11

 Write an addition and subtraction calculation for each pair of numbers. Show all your working.

 Example

65 and 24

65 + 24 =   65 – 24 =
65 + 20 = 85   65 – 20 = 45
85 + 4 = 89   45 – 4 = 41

a 54 16

b 36 12

c 46 22

d 69 21

e 57 33

f 85 15

g 86 32

h 67 15

 Make up some addition and subtraction calculations involving pairs of two-digit numbers for yourself to work out mentally. Your teacher will tell you how many calculations to make up.

Wash day calculations

● **Add or subtract mentally combinations of one-digit and two-digit numbers**

① Write addition calculations using the numbers on the shirts. Your teacher will tell you how many calculations to do.

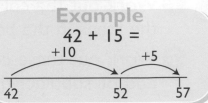

Example

42 + 15 =

```
      +10         +5
   ⌒‾‾‾‾‾⌒   ⌒‾‾‾⌒
  42          52    57
```

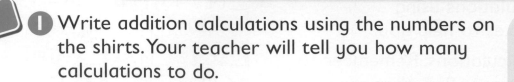

12 23 42 14 30 15 32 43

② Write subtraction calculations using the numbers on the trousers. Your teacher will tell you how many calculations to do.

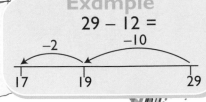

Example

29 − 12 =

```
        −2        −10
     ⌒‾‾‾⌒   ⌒‾‾‾‾‾⌒
   17     19          29
```

17 12 13 14 28 29 30 19

Choosing two numbers each time from the washing line, make up addition and subtraction calculations. Your teacher will tell you how many addition and subtraction calculations to do.

43 25 64 78 71 13 96 82 68 57 39 47

① Write 5 calculations adding 2 two-digit numbers that equal 85.

② Write 5 calculations involving 2 two-digit numbers that have a difference of 16.

Remember when subtracting to take the smaller number away from the larger number.

The 6 times table (1)

● **Begin to know the 6 times table**

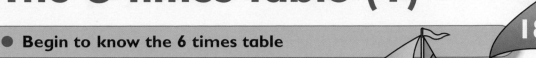

Double each of these numbers.

Complete each multiplication fact for the 3 times table on the outside of the card.

Then work out the answer for the 6 times table on the inside of the card, by doubling the answer to the 3 times table.

a
4 × 3
4 × 6

b
3 × 3
3 × 6

c
8 × 3
8 × 6

d
9 × 3
9 × 6

e
5 × 3
5 × 6

f
7 × 3
7 × 6

g
2 × 3
2 × 6

h
6 × 3
6 × 6

i
10 × 3
10 × 6

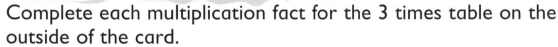

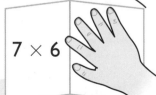

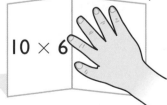

Copy and complete.

a 30 ÷ 3 =   **b** 15 ÷ 3 =   **c** 9 ÷ 3 =
d 12 ÷ 3 =   **e** 24 ÷ 3 =   **f** 21 ÷ 3 =
g 18 ÷ 3 =   **h** 6 ÷ 3 =   **i** 27 ÷ 3 =

The 6 times table (2)

● **Begin to know the 6 times table**

 For each of the following arrays write two multiplication calculations.

Example

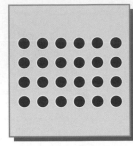

$3 \times 6 = 18$

$6 \times 3 = 18$

a 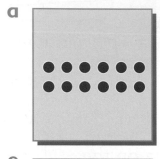 b 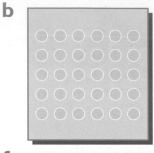 c 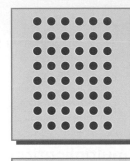 d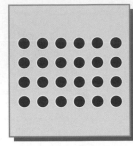

e 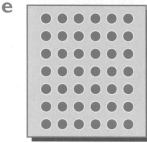 f 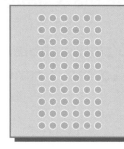 g 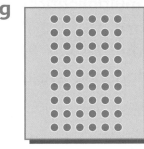 h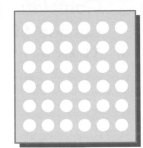

Use your knowledge of the key facts to work out the answers to these multiplication and division facts for the 6 times table.

1 a $5 \times 6 =$ b $7 \times 6 =$ c $9 \times 6 =$
  d $6 \times 6 =$ e $10 \times 6 =$ f $8 \times 6 =$
  g $2 \times 6 =$ h $4 \times 6 =$ i $3 \times 6 =$

2 a $24 \div 6 =$ b $48 \div 6 =$ c $60 \div 6 =$
  d $18 \div 6 =$ e $30 \div 6 =$ f $54 \div 6 =$
  g $36 \div 6 =$ h $42 \div 6 =$ i $12 \div 6 =$

 Look at the pairs of multiplication calculations you wrote out for the ▢ activity. For each pair write down the two related division calculations.

Example

$3 \times 6 = 18$ $18 \div 3 = 6$

$6 \times 3 = 18$ $18 \div 6 = 3$

Fruit problems

● **Know multiplication facts for the 2, 3, 4, 5, 6 and 10 times tables**

 apples £5    lemons £2    grapes £4    mangoes £10    oranges £3

Look at the price on each box of fruit then work out the calculations below.

apples

Buy	×£5
6	£30
3	£15
9	
4	

lemons

Buy	×£2
8	
7	
6	
9	

grapes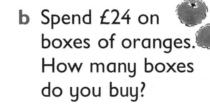

Buy	×£4
3	
5	
8	
6	

mangoes

Buy	×£10
7	
5	
3	
8	

oranges

Buy	×£3
6	
9	
7	
3	

Work out the answers to these word problems.

a Buy 7 boxes of apples. How much do you spend?

b Spend £24 on boxes of oranges. How many boxes do you buy?

c You have £28. How many boxes of grapes can you buy?

d Buy 9 boxes of mangoes. How much money do you need?

e You have £10. How many boxes of lemons can you buy?

f How much does it cost to buy 8 boxes of apples?

Work out the answers to these word problems. Show all your working.

a Buy 5 boxes of mangoes, 3 boxes of oranges and 4 boxes of grapes. How much does it cost altogether?

b You have £50. Do you have enough money to buy 7 boxes of oranges and 2 boxes of grapes? Explain how you know.

10 times, 100 times

● **Multiply numbers by 10 or 100**

	×10	×100
1	10	100
2	20	200
3		
4		
5		
6		
7		
8		
9		
10		

1. Josh and Sam drew a table to help them see what happens when a number is multiplied by 10 and 100. Copy the table and help them to finish it.

2. What pattern can you see when a number is multiplied by 10?

3. What pattern can you see when a number is multiplied by 100?

Example

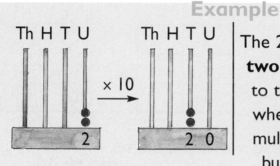

The 2 moves **one** place to the left when it is multiplied by 10.

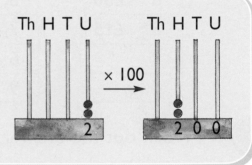

The 2 moves **two** places to the left when it is multiplied by 100.

Write a multiplication number sentence for each picture.

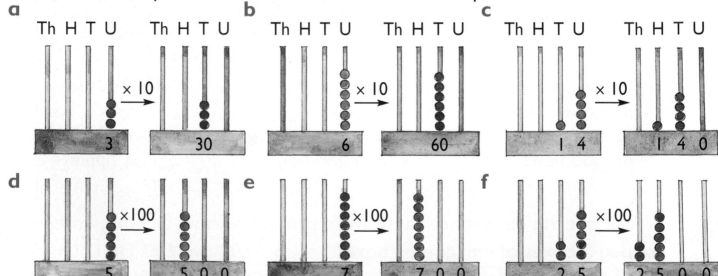

a
b
c
d
e
f

Explain what happens when a number is divided by 10 or 100. Provide examples to illustrate your explanation.

What was the question?

● **Solve mathematical puzzles**

The answer is

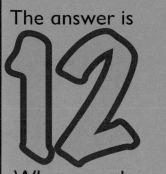

12

What was the question?

a How many different addition calculations can you write with an answer of 12?

b How many different subtraction calculations can you write with an answer of 12?

The answer is

24

What was the question?

a Can you write at least 24 different addition and subtraction calculations with the answer 24?

b How many multiplication calculations can you write with the answer 24?

c How many different calculations can you write with an answer of 24 using two of these operations in each one: +, −, × or ÷?

The answer is

36

What was the question?

a Can you write at least 36 different addition and subtraction calculations with the answer 36?

b How many multiplication calculations can you write with the answer 36?

c How many different calculations can you write with an answer of 36 using two of these operations in each one: +, −, × or ÷?

 How many different division calculations can you write with answers of 12, 24 or 36?

Delicious problems

● **Solve one-step and two-step problems involving money**

Tom has £1 to spend at the mini-market.

1 How much would he pay for crisps and a chocolate bar?

2 How much would he pay for a drink and bubble gum?

3 Tom buys a bag of crisps and pays with a 50p coin. How much change does he get?

4 Tom buys a drink and pays with a £1 coin. How much change does he get?

5 What is the cost of two packets of bubblegum?

6 How much change does Tom get from £2 if he buys 2 chocolate bars?

Jim has £4.00 to spend at the newsagent and Rose has £4.50.

1 How much more does Rose have to spend than Jim?

2 Rose spends half of her money on a game. How much does she spend?

3 Rose is given £2.45 more. How much does she have now?

4 Jim buys some pencils and a packet of stickers. He pays with a £2 coin. How much change does he get?

5 Rose buys 2 packets of pens and pays with 3 coins. Which coins did she use?

6 Jim buys stickers, pens and pencils. How much does he spend?

Write 3 two-step problems using the prices on this page. Swap your problems with a friend and work out the answers to their problems. Swap back and check.

Folding fractions

● **Identify and estimate fractions of shapes**

Investigate how many ways you can fold each of these shapes in half. Draw each of your shapes and show your folds as dotted lines. Write the fractions.

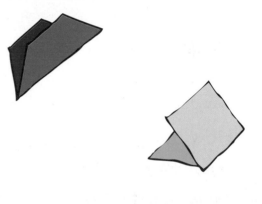

You need:

● ruler

● paper shapes like these

I folded my square in half.

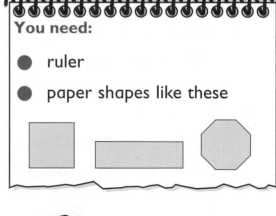

Investigate how many ways you can fold each of these shapes in quarters. Draw each of your shapes and show your folds as dotted lines. Write the fractions. Also draw the folds you try that do not work.

You need:

● ruler

● paper shapes like these

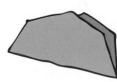

Investigate how many ways you can fold a circle in half. Explain your findings using words and diagrams.

Find the fraction

● **Identify and estimate fractions of shapes**

1 Write the fraction of each shape that has been shaded.

a    b    c    d

e 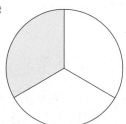   f 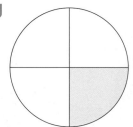   g 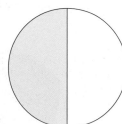   h

HINT

First count how many parts the shape is divided into.

2 How many parts of each shape are not shaded? Write this as a fraction.

1 Draw 3 rectangles like this.

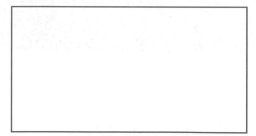

a Divide the first rectangle into thirds.

b Divide the second rectangle into fifths.

c Divide the third rectangle into tenths.

d Shade 1 part of each shape and label the fraction.

You need:
● ruler

2 Write down the fraction of each shape that has been shaded.

a 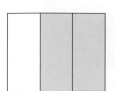   b 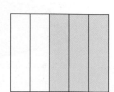   c 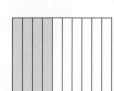   d    e

 Draw 4 different shapes to show the fraction $\frac{3}{8}$.

Patterns of 3

● **Describe and continue patterns to solve a puzzle**

Investigate multiples of 3 to 50.

● Starting from 0 use the number line below to make jumps of 3 to 50.

● Write the multiples of 3 under each other.

● For each number add the digits until you have a single-digit number.

● Write about any patterns you notice.

Investigation

1 Starting from 1, count in 3s up to about 60. Write the numbers under each other. Add the digits in each of the numbers. Continue adding the digits until you have a single-digit number. What do you notice?

2 Starting from 2 and counting in 3s up to about 60, write the numbers as before. What do you notice?

> For a multiple of 3
> I can add the digits and
> end up with a 3, 6 or 9.
> 24 ➤ 2 + 4 = 6
> 39 ➤ 3 + 9 = 12
> ➤ 1 + 2 = 3

0 1 2 3 4 5 6 7 8 9 10 11 12 13 14 15 16 17 18 19 20 21 22 23 24 25 26 27 28 29 30 31 32 33 34 35 36 37 38 39 40 41 42 43 44 45 46 47 48 49 50

What if you start from 120 and count on in 3s? Will the pattern work for three-digit numbers?

Investigating 2s, 3s, 4s and 5s

● **Find the pattern to solve the puzzle**

The children in Year 3 carried out an investigation. They added 3s and 5s to make all of the numbers between 10 and 20.
Here are their results.

Continue the investigation to see if you can make the numbers between 21 and 30.

Year 3 Investigation

10 ➞	5 + 5
11 ➞	3 + 3 + 5
12 ➞	3 + 3 + 3 + 3
13 ➞	3 + 5 + 5
14 ➞	3 + 3 + 3 + 5
15 ➞	5 + 5 + 5
16 ➞	5 + 5 + 3 + 3
17 ➞	3 + 3 + 3 + 3 + 5
18 ➞	3 + 5 + 5 + 5
19 ➞	5 + 5 + 3 + 3 + 3
20 ➞	5 + 5 + 5 + 5

① Investigation

What numbers can you make by adding 3s and 4s together?

Can you make all of the numbers between 7 and 30?

② Investigation

What numbers can you make by adding 2s and 5s together?

Can you make all of the numbers between 7 and 30?

Miss Carruth has 20p and 50p coins in her purse. What amounts to £2 can she make?

Finding multiples

● Recognise multiples of 2, 3, 4, 5 and 10, up to the tenth multiple

Inside the bag, lots of numbers were found.
Sort them into multiples of 2, 5 and 10.

Draw your own Venn Diagrams like the ones below.
Sort the numbers 1 to 50 to match the labels.
Write any numbers that belong in both sets in the middle.

a
multiples of 2   multiples of 5

b
multiples of 5   multiples of 10

c
multiples of 3   multiples of 5

d
multiples of 3   multiples of 10

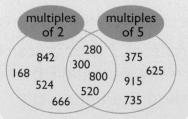

Draw your own Venn diagrams like the ones in the ● section above. For each Venn diagram, write four three-digit numbers in each section.

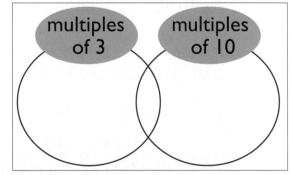

Example

multiples of 2   multiples of 5

168
842   280
       300
524   800   375
       520   915   625
  666   735

19

Reviewing multiplication facts

● Know by heart the multiplication facts for the 2, 3, 4, 5, 6 and 10 times tables

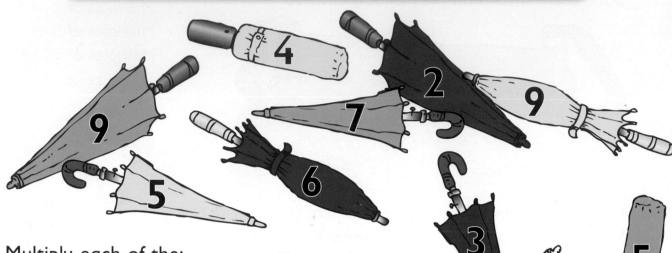

Multiply each of the:

– **red** umbrellas by 2
– **blue** umbrellas by 5
– **yellow** umbrellas by 10

Example

$4 \times 2 = 8$

Multiply each of the:

– **red** umbrellas by 3
– **blue** umbrellas by 4
– **yellow** umbrellas by 6

Example

$4 \times 3 = 12$

Use the clues to find the number.

a A multiple of 6 that is between 20 and 30.

b A two-digit number greater than 50, which is a multiple of 5 and also a multiple of 9.

c The nearest multiple of 4 to 45.

d A multiple of 3 that is less than 50, with the tens digit that is 1 more than the units digit.

e The first three-digit multiple of 5.

f A multiple of 6 that is greater than 15 but less than 20.

g The smallest number which is a multiple of 2, a multiple of 3 and also a multiple of 4.

h The tenth multiple of 6.

Reviewing division facts

● Know division facts related to the 2, 3, 4, 5, 6 and 10 times tables

Copy and complete.

a 28 ÷ 4 = ☐   b 12 ÷ 3 = ☐   c 16 ÷ 2 = ☐   d 30 ÷ 10 = ☐

e 16 ÷ 4 = ☐   f 36 ÷ 6 = ☐   g 25 ÷ 5 = ☐   h 20 ÷ 2 = ☐

i 45 ÷ 5 = ☐   j 24 ÷ 3 = ☐   k 36 ÷ 4 = ☐   l 15 ÷ 3 = ☐

m 60 ÷ 10 = ☐   n 8 ÷ 4 = ☐   o 9 ÷ 3 = ☐   p 42 ÷ 6 = ☐

Choose a shell from each sandcastle to make a division calculation. Write the answer. Do this 20 times.

Example

24 ÷ 3 = 8

☐☐₂₁ means find part of the square where the product is 21, i.e. ☐7☐3☐

Now find these parts of the square.

a ☐☐₈₀   b ☐☐₃₀   c ☐☐₃₂   d ☐☐₁₄   e ☐☐₃₆

f ☐☐₄₀   g ☐☐₁₈   h ☐☐₂₄   i ☐☐₅₄   j ☐☐₄₂

2	3	5	6	2
7	3	8	4	9
3	5	6	8	10
4	8	5	7	4
10	9	7	2	6

Reviewing multiplication and division facts (1)

● Know multiplication facts for the 2, 3, 4, 5, 6 and 10 times tables and the related division facts

 Copy and complete.

a $3 \times \bigcirc = 12$ b $\bigcirc \times 3 = 27$ c $\bigcirc \times 4 = 16$ d $8 \times \bigcirc = 80$

e $\bigcirc \times 4 = 24$ f $7 \times \bigcirc = 42$ g $8 \times \bigcirc = 40$ h $\bigcirc \times 2 = 18$

i $\bigcirc \times 5 = 25$ j $\bigcirc \times 2 = 8$ k $\bigcirc \times 4 = 36$ l $\bigcirc \times 3 = 24$

m $6 \times \bigcirc = 60$ n $8 \times \bigcirc = 32$ o $\bigcirc \times 3 = 21$ p $9 \times \bigcirc = 63$

 Copy and complete.

1 a $16 \div \bigcirc = 4$ b $\bigcirc \div 5 = 7$ c $\bigcirc \div 6 = 6$ d $40 \div \bigcirc = 8$

e $\bigcirc \div 4 = 7$ f $16 \div \bigcirc = 8$ g $\bigcirc \div 3 = 4$ h $30 \div \bigcirc = 3$

i $18 \div \bigcirc = 9$ j $\bigcirc \div 4 = 4$ k $24 \div \bigcirc = 8$ l $15 \div \bigcirc = 5$

m $60 \div \bigcirc = 6$ n $9 \div \bigcirc = 3$ o $36 \div \bigcirc = 9$ p $\bigcirc \div 6 = 9$

2 For each set of three numbers, write two multiplication and two division calculations.

a 9, 4, 36   b 8, 3, 24   c 6, 7, 42   d 5, 9, 45

 Copy and complete the table.

$2 \times 10 =$ $14 \div 2 =$

×		10			6
	32				24
2			14		
			35		
				54	
3	24			27	

What's the problem?

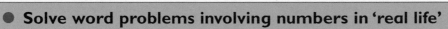

● **Solve word problems involving numbers in 'real life'**

Write the answer to these multiplication and division facts.

a 20 ÷ 5 = ☐

4 × 6 = ☐

12 ÷ 2 = ☐

35 ÷ 5 = ☐

b 16 ÷ 4 = ☐

9 × 3 = ☐

4 × 2 = ☐

25 ÷ 5 = ☐

c 10 × 10 = ☐

40 ÷ 4 = ☐

18 ÷ 6 = ☐

12 ÷ 3 = ☐

Work out the answers to these problems. Show all your working.

a A chocolate bar costs 5p. How many can you buy for 45p?

b Sam gets £5 pocket money each week. He wants to buy a football for £20 and a computer game for £25. How many weeks will it take him to save enough money?

c Put 24 cakes into bags. How many cakes in each bag?

d 3 biscuits cost 27p altogether. How much did each cost?

e How much more does it cost to buy 8 books for £5 each than 9 calculators for £3 each?

f 8 children ate 3 doughnuts each. How many doughnuts did they eat altogether?

g James and Mary collect stamps. James has 15 and Mary has 13. They put 7 stamps on each page of their albums. How many pages do they use?

h Roses cost £15 for 5. Daffodils cost £8 for 4. Sunflowers cost £20 for 4. Mrs Singh buys 1 of each flower. How much does she spend?

Write 3 two-step word problems for a friend to solve using money as the theme.

Shipwreck solids

● **Name and describe 3-D solids**

Some shapes from the wreck are floating in the sea.
Use the clues and name these shapes.

a I have – 6 faces
– 8 vertices
– 12 edges

I am a ——————.

b I have – 1 curved face
– 2 circular faces
– 2 curved edges

I am a ——————.

Copy the clues and work out the name of each solid.

Shape a
2 identical hexagonal faces
6 rectangular faces
12 vertices

Shape b
a curved face and a flat face
a circular base
no vertices

Shape c
4 rectangular faces
2 square faces
8 vertices

Shape d
2 identical triangular faces at
opposite ends and all the other
faces are rectangles

Shape e
no edges
no vertices
a curved surface only

Write 3 clues for a square-based pyramid.

Creating 2-D shapes

● **Name and describe 2-D shapes**

You need:

● 2 rectangles
  10 cm × 5 cm

● ruler

● scissors

Work with
a partner.

Cut one of the
rectangles in half.

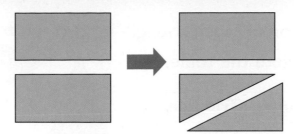

Use the rectangle and both right-angled triangles to make these shapes.

1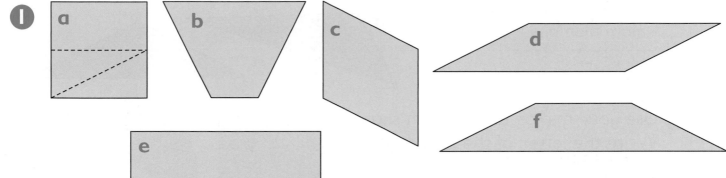

a   b   c   d   e   f

2 Name the shapes which have right angles.

Work with a partner.

Make these shapes with the rectangle and the two right-angled triangles.

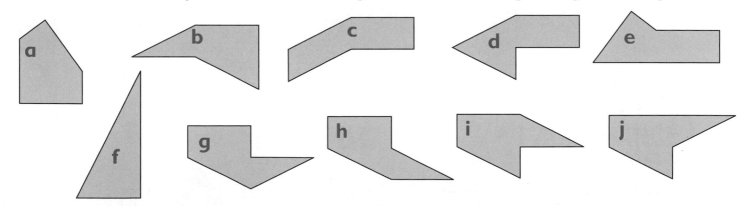

a   b   c   d   e   f   g   h   i   j

Copy and complete the
table for the shapes in the
section.

Property	Letter of shape
with 1 right angle	b,
with more than 1 right angle	

25

Symmetry in shapes

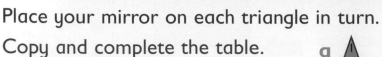
● Recognise lines of symmetry in shapes and recognise shapes with no lines of symmetry

You need:
●●● mirror

Place your mirror on each triangle in turn.
Copy and complete the table.

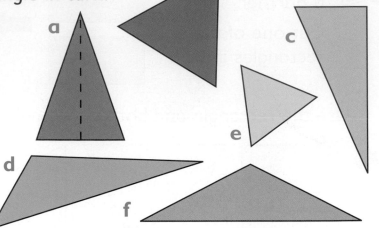

Lines of symmetry	Triangle
none	
one	a,
more than one	

1 Use your mirror to test each shape.
Write the letter of the shapes which have:
i   no lines of symmetry
ii one line of symmetry
iii more than one line of symmetry.

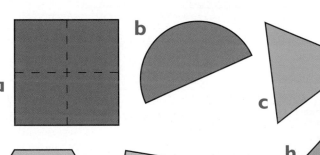

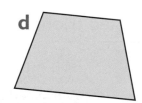

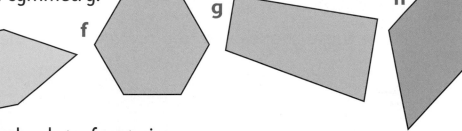

2 Find a way to read these back-to-front signs.

Design a mirror sign with a printed message.

Mirror symmetry

● **Reflect a shape when the mirror line is along one of its sides**

You need:
●●● mirror

Place your mirror along one edge to make these shapes whole.
Name each shape.

a
b
c
d
e
f
g

Place your mirror along one edge to make these shapes whole.

Name each 2-D shape. Then draw it in your exercise book.

Example
← Mirror line
Rectangle

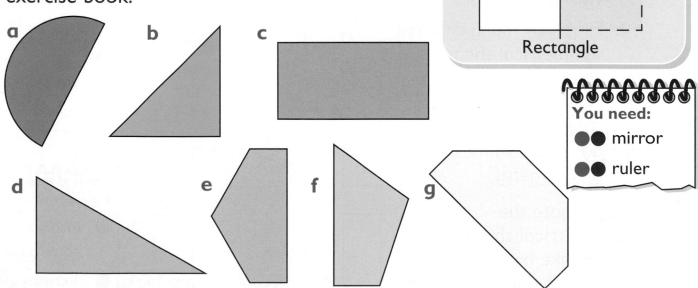

a
b
c
d
e
f
g

You need:
●● mirror
●● ruler

How many different shapes can you make with shape **g** and a mirror?

27

Symmetry puzzles

● **Draw symmetrical shapes**

a Join the square tiles to make these shapes.

b Join 2 or 3 shapes to make these symmetrical patterns.

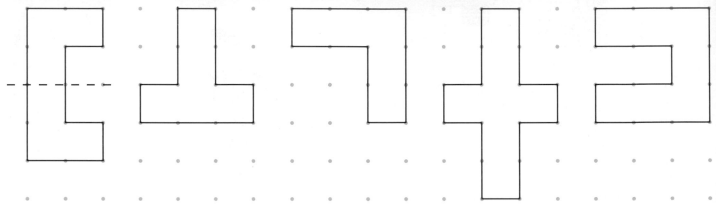

c Draw each shape on 1 cm squared dot paper and mark the line of symmetry.

Work with a partner.

a Make two T-shapes with your square tiles.

b Find how many different symmetrical shapes you can make by joining two T-shapes. Record each shape on 1 cm squared dot paper. Mark the line of symmetry.

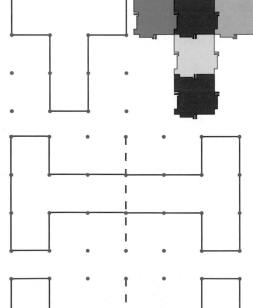

Investigate the symmetrical shapes you can make by joining pairs of L-shapes. Record each shape on 1 cm squared dot paper. Mark the line of symmetry.

Easter egg weights

● **Know how many grams are the same as a kilogram**

These children each found $\frac{1}{2}$ kg of eggs in the Easter Egg Hunt.
Copy and complete the table to show the weights of the eggs that each child found.

Child	200 g	100 g
Keri	2	1
Kevin		3
Kitty		

I found two 200 g eggs and one 100 g egg. That's 500 g altogether.

These children each found 1 kg of eggs in the Easter Egg Hunt. Copy and complete the table.

Child	500 g	200 g	100 g
Abby	1	2	1
Bert	1		3
Cindy	0	4	
Dan	0		6
Eli		0	0
Fran	0		0
Jill	1	0	
Hetty	0		4
Iyaz	0	1	
Jenny	0	0	

Example

Abby found:
500 g + 200 g + 200 g + 100 g = 1000 g
or = 1 kg

Rob found $1\frac{1}{2}$ kg of eggs.
The heaviest egg weighed 500 g.
Find three different combinations of eggs whose total weight is $1\frac{1}{2}$ kg.

Ready, steady, cookery

● **Solve word problems involving grams**

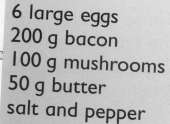

Scrambled Eggs
(serves 4)

6 large eggs
200 g bacon
100 g mushrooms
50 g butter
salt and pepper

 Look at the Scrambled Eggs recipe for 4 people.

a Write a Scrambled Eggs recipe for 2 people.

b Now write the recipe for 8 people.

 These recipes are for 4 people.

Seafood Pasta
(serves 4)

400 g pasta
300 g mussels
200 g prawns
500 g plum tomatoes
20 g chilli pepper
100 g parmesan cheese
2 cloves of garlic

Singapore Rice Noodles
(serves 4)

200 g rice noodles
125 g cooked chicken
50 g prawns
100 g beansprouts
30 g onion
60 g oil

I opened a 500 g pack of rice noodles to cook the meal for eight people. What is the weight of the noodles left?

a Write the Seafood Pasta recipe for 2 people.

b Write the Singapore Rice Noodles recipe for 8 people.

 Write a Seafood Pasta recipe for 6 people.

Clock face times

● **Read the time to the nearest 5 minutes on a clock with hands and a digital 12-hour clock**

Write these times.

a

b

c

d

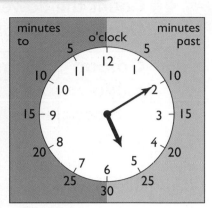

e

f
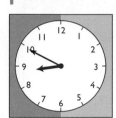

g

h

① Look at this clock. Copy and complete the sentences.

a The time is ——— minutes ——— 3.

b In another ——— minutes it will be $\frac{1}{4}$ to 3.

c In 25 minutes it will be ——— .

② Look at the 8 clocks in the  section. Write what time each clock showed:

a 10 minutes ago

b 20 minutes ago

c 2 hours ago

③ Look at the 8 clocks in the  section again. This time write what time each clock will show in:

a 10 minutes' time

b 25 minutes' time

c 1 hour's time

You need:

● RCM: Blank Clockfaces

 Use RCM: Blank Clockfaces to show these times.

a 15 minutes past 4   b 10 minutes to 8   c 25 minutes past 10
d 5 minutes to 5   e 20 minutes past 2   f 30 minutes past 1
g 3:20   h 5:10   i 2:40
j 6:15   k 1:05   l 10:35

Flower charts

1 Count the flowers of each colour.
Copy and complete the table.

Colour	Number
Red	
Yellow	
Blue	
Orange	

2 Copy and complete the bar chart.

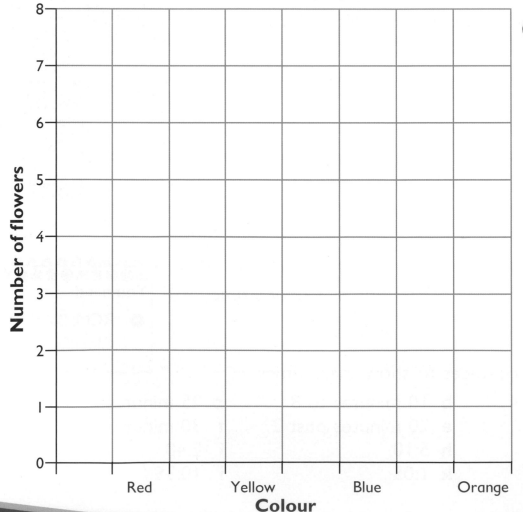

Colour of flowers

You need:
● ● ● squared paper
● ● ● ruler
● ● ● coloured pencils

1 Count the cans of each type.
Copy and complete the table.

Can	Number
Cola	
Lemonade	
Orange	
Cherry	

2 Copy and complete the bar chart.

Cans of drink

3 Write 3 sentences about the information presented in the bar chart.

 Draw a pictogram for the data in the ● section.

33

Collins Close

Make a tally mark to record all the things you can see in Collins Close. Count the tally marks and write the totals.

	Tally	Total
Bus stop		
House		
Car		
Zebra crossing		
People		

1 Copy and complete the bar chart to record all the things you can see in Collins Close, and then answer these questions.

You need:
- squared paper
- ruler
- coloured pencils

   a What does the tallest bar show?

   b Are there more houses or cars? How many more?

   c How many bus stops and cars are there altogether?

2 Write 2 sentences about the information displayed in the bar chart.

Collins Close

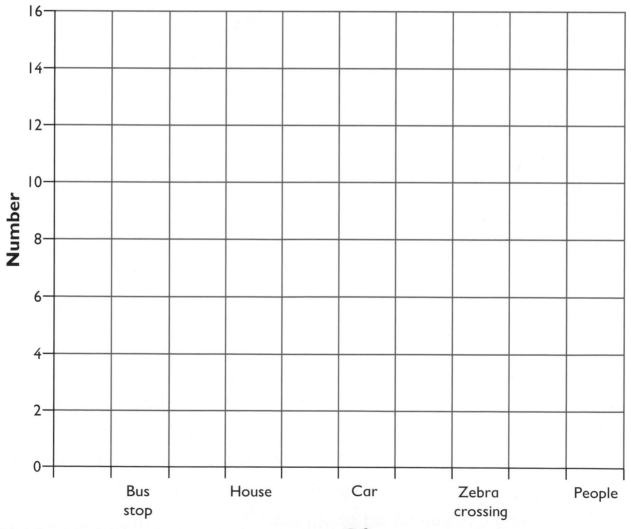

 Draw a pictogram for the data in the section.

Pet names pictograms

● **Show information in a pictogram where a picture represents two votes**

Some children voted for the rabbit name they prefer.

Name	Votes
Flopsy	8
Long Ears	6
Bobtail	2
Bugs	12

1 **a** How many children voted for Long Ears?

b How many more children voted for Bugs than Bobtail?

c How many children voted for Bobtail or Flopsy?

d What is the most popular name?

2 Copy and complete this pictogram.
Draw 🐰 to stand for two names.

You need:
● squared paper
● ruler

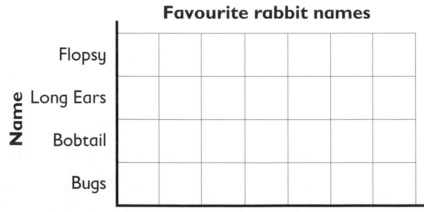

Favourite rabbit names

Name

Flopsy

Long Ears

Bobtail

Bugs

Number of votes

Key

3 Use the information in the completed pictogram to answer these questions.

a What is the least popular name? How does your pictogram show this?

b How many more children voted for Bugs than Flopsy?

c How many children voted altogether?

4 Write a sentence about the information displayed in your pictogram.

A pet club voted for the dog name they prefer.

1 **a** How many people voted for Patch?

b How many people voted for Patch or Chipper?

Name	Votes
Chipper	2
Patch	5
Lassie	13
Spot	10

c How many people voted altogether?

d What is the most popular name?

2 Copy and complete this pictogram.
Choose your own picture to stand for two names.

You need:
● squared paper
● ruler

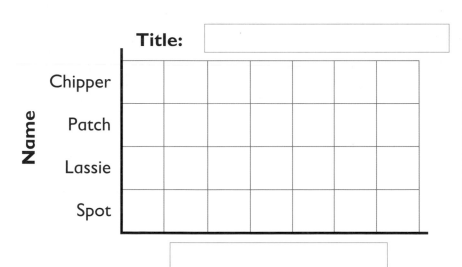

Title:

Name

Chipper

Patch

Lassie

Spot

Key

3 Use the information from the completed pictogram to answer these questions.

a What is the least popular name? How does your pictogram show this?

b How many more children voted for Lassie than Patch?

c How many children did not vote for Spot?

4 Write a sentence about the information displayed in your pictogram.

You need:
● squared paper
● ruler
● coloured pencils

Draw a bar chart to show the data in the section.

Holiday rock

● **Show information using pictograms, tables and tally charts**

1 Copy the pictogram. Choose a picture to stand for two sticks of rock.

Count the sticks for each name.

Complete the key.

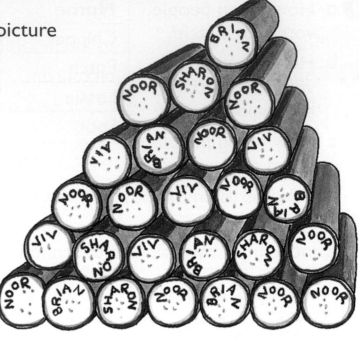

Names on rock

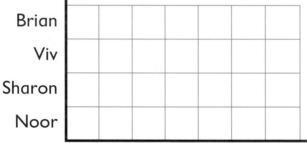

Number of sticks

Key

You need:
● squared paper
● ruler

2 Use the information in the pictogram to answer these questions.

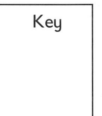

   a What is the most common name?

   b How many sticks has Brian?

   c How many sticks has Viv?

   d Who has more sticks Sharon or Noor? How many more?

   e How many sticks are there altogether?

3 Write a sentence about the information displayed in your pictogram.

1 Copy this tally chart.

Working in groups, pass round a bag of counters.

Take turns to take one and say its colour.

Make a tally mark next to each colour.

Colour	Tally
Red	

2 Copy and complete the pictogram.

Choose a picture to stand for two tally marks.

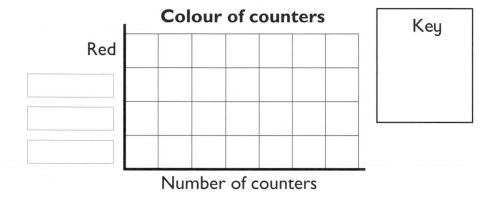

Colour of counters

Red

Number of counters

Key

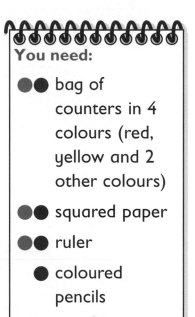

You need:

●● bag of counters in 4 colours (red, yellow and 2 other colours)

●● squared paper

●● ruler

● coloured pencils

3 Use the information in the pictogram to answer these questions.

a What is the most common colour?

b How many red counters are there?

c Which are there more of – red or yellow counters?

d How many counters are not red?

e How many counters altogether?

4 Write 2 sentences about the information displayed in your pictogram.

Draw a bar chart for the data in the ⬤ section.

Parachute Carroll diagrams

1 Look at the parachutes on both pages. Copy the Carroll diagram.

2 Write the numbers on the diagram.

3 How many numbers are even?

4 How many numbers are not even?

Parachute numbers	
Even	**Not even**

1 Copy the Carroll diagram.

2 Think of all the odd numbers up to 20. Write them on the diagram.

Odd numbers up to 20	
One-digit	**More than one digit**

3 Copy the Carroll diagram below.

4 Think of all the multiples of 5 up to 100. Write them on the diagram.

Multiples of 5 up to 100	
Odd	**Not odd**

5 Use your completed diagram for question 4 to answer these questions.

   a How many multiples of 5 are odd?

   b How many multiples of 5 are not odd?

   c How many multiples of 5 are there from 5 to 100?

Work in pairs. Each person writes down 10 numbers between 1 and 100. Decide how to sort them into two sets. Draw a Carroll diagram to show how you sorted the numbers.

Dice Carroll diagrams

● Sort objects using a Carroll diagram

Work in pairs. Each person copies the Carroll diagram. Hold a handful of cubes behind your back. Your partner has to guess how many are in your hand: 'less than 5' or '5 or more'. They make a cross in their Carroll diagram. Have ten guesses each.

Less than 5	5 or more

You need:

● about 10 small cubes

Work in pairs. Each person copies the Carroll diagram and writes both names. Take turns to roll the dice. Write the number in the correct section of the Carroll diagram. Have ten rolls each. Who rolled more sixes?

You need:
● 1–6 dice

	Six	Not a six
Name		
Name		

Copy the Carroll diagram.

	Less than 5	**5 or more**
Odd	○	○
Even	○	○

Roll the dice 20 times. Write each number in the appropriate section of each circle on the Carroll diagram.

Write the total number of occurrences in each circle on the Carroll diagram.

You need:
● 0–9 dice

Youth Club improvements

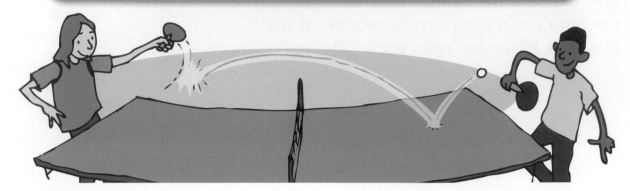

Templeton Youth Club raised £1000 for improvements. Each senior member voted for one improvement. The bar chart shows the results.

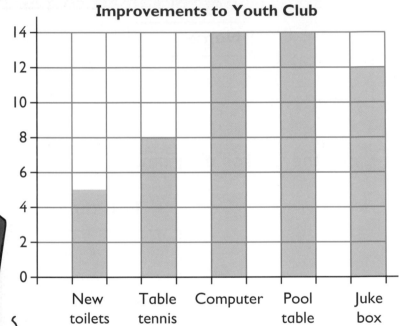

Improvements to Youth Club

① How many people voted for table tennis?

② Which was the most popular improvement?

③ Copy and complete the table.

Improvement	Votes
New toilets	
Table tennis	
Computer	
Pool table	
Jukebox	

The junior members also voted. Their results are shown here.

Improvement	Votes
New toilets	2
Table tennis	4
Computer	8
Pool table	5
Jukebox	7

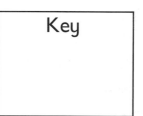

You need:
● squared paper
● ruler

1 Copy and complete the pictogram.

Improvements to Youth Club

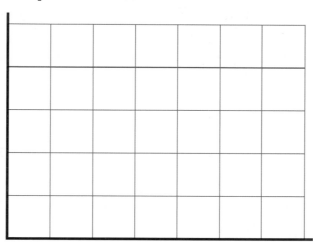

Improvements

New toilets
Table tennis
Computer
Pool table
Jukebox

Votes

Key

2 How are the senior and junior results different? Write two sentences.

1 Combine the junior and senior votes into a copy of this table.

Improvement	Votes
New toilets	
Table tennis	
Computer	
Pool table	
Jukebox	

2 Draw a bar chart for the data.

3 Draw a pictogram for the data.

4 Which improvement is the most popular overall?

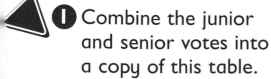

You need:
● squared paper
● ruler
● colouring pencils

Add it

● **Use written methods to add combinations of two-digit and three-digit numbers**

① Work out these addition calculations. Show all your working.

a 32 + 16 = ☐   **b** 25 + 31 = ☐   **c** 12 + 36 = ☐

d 45 + 23 = ☐   **e** 37 + 22 = ☐   **f** 56 + 41 = ☐

g 63 + 29 = ☐   **h** 54 + 38 = ☐   **i** 57 + 34 = ☐

j 52 + 29 = ☐   **k** 68 + 17 = ☐   **l** 87 + 23 = ☐

m 54 + 65 = ☐   **n** 84 + 73 = ☐   **o** 32 + 94 = ☐

② Choose two calculations and explain your method in words.

① **a** 83 + 49 = ☐   **b** 76 + 57 = ☐   **c** 91 + 68 = ☐

d 134 + 42 = ☐   **e** 33 + 161 = ☐   **f** 25 + 153 = ☐

g 127 + 48 = ☐   **h** 56 + 118 = ☐   **i** 28 + 157 = ☐

j 143 + 59 = ☐   **k** 121 + 79 = ☐   **l** 149 + 37 = ☐

m 64 + 173 = ☐   **n** 156 + 82 = ☐   **o** 184 + 57 = ☐

p 39 + 193 = ☐   **q** 87 + 158 = ☐   **r** 177 + 66 = ☐

② Choose one two-digit plus two-digit calculation, and one three-digit plus two-digit calculation and explain your methods.

What do you think the boy and girl in the picture are saying to each other about their methods?

Creepy crawlie difference

● Use written methods to subtract combinations of two-digit and three-digit numbers

Example

$106 - 97 = 9$

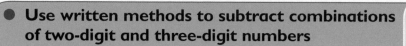

Use the snake line to work out the difference between each pair of numbers. Show your working on an empty number line.

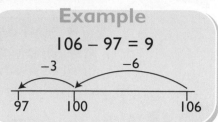

a  $102 - 98 =$

b $104 - 97 =$

c $106 - 98 =$

d $101 - 95 =$

e $103 - 97 =$

f $105 - 95 =$

Find the difference between each pair of numbers to work out the calculations. Show your working on an empty number line.

a $303 - 291 =$

b $104 - 82 =$

c $86 - 67 =$

d $212 - 194 =$

e $205 - 99 =$

f $301 - 193 =$

g $414 - 389 =$

h $502 - 199 =$

 Explain what the term 'difference between' means.

Juicy fractions

- **Find unit fractions of numbers and quantities**
- **Begin to recognise simple fractions that are several parts of a whole, such as $\frac{3}{4}$, $\frac{2}{3}$ or $\frac{3}{10}$**

 1 Write the fraction of juice left in each carton.

full

a b c d e

2 How much juice is left in each carton? The labels tell you how much they hold when they are full.

a b c d e f

200 ml   500 ml   400 ml   120 ml   60 ml   90 ml

 1 Write the fraction of juice that has been drunk from each carton.

a b c d e

2 How much does each container hold when it is full? The labels show you how much is in each carton now.

  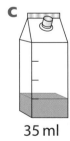 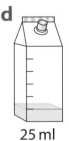 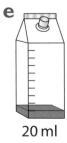 

a b c d e f

125 ml   60 ml   35 ml   25 ml   20 ml   15 ml

Calculate these fractions of numbers.

Example

$\frac{1}{10}$ of 30 = 3

30 ÷ 10 = 3

a $\frac{1}{10}$ of 50 = ☐ $\frac{1}{10}$ of 20 = ☐ $\frac{1}{10}$ of 40 = ☐

b $\frac{1}{5}$ of 50 = ☐ $\frac{1}{5}$ of 20 = ☐ $\frac{1}{5}$ of 40 = ☐

c $\frac{1}{3}$ of 60 = ☐ $\frac{1}{3}$ of 99 = ☐ $\frac{1}{3}$ of 330 = ☐

Multiplying a 'teens' number

- Multiply a 'teens' number by a one-digit number

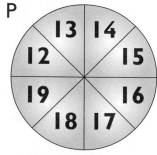

- One person is Player A, the other Player B.
- Take turns to:
  - Spin spinner P.
  - ▢ Spin spinner Q ● Spin spinner R
  - ▲ Spin spinner S.
  - Multiply the two numbers together.
  - If the answer is one the numbers on your number strip, place a counter on the number. If not, do nothing.
- The winner is the first person to complete a row of 8 counters on their number strip.

Example

18 × 6 = (10 × 6) + (8 × 6)
= 60 + 48
= 108

You need:

●●● paper clip (per pair)

●●● pencil (per pair)

●●● 24 counters (per pair)

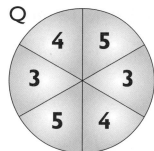 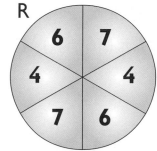

P: 13 14 12 15 19 16 18 17

Q: 4 5 3 3 5 4

R: 6 7 4 4 7 6

S: 8 9 7 7 9 8

Player A	36	45	48	51	56	57	60	64	75	76	80	95
Player B	39	42	48	52	54	60	65	68	70	72	85	90
Player A	56	60	68	72	78	84	91	96	105	108	119	126
Player B	48	52	64	76	72	84	90	98	102	112	114	133
Player A	84	98	104	108	112	120	126	133	135	144	153	162
Player B	91	96	105	112	117	119	126	128	135	144	152	171

Dividing a two-digit number

● Divide a two-digit number by a one-digit number

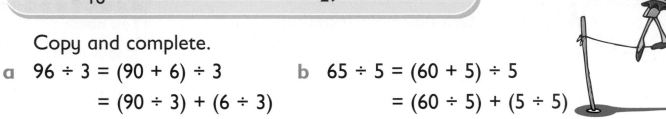

Example

$72 \div 4 = (40 + 32) \div 4$ $87 \div 3 = (60 + 27) \div 3$

$\quad\quad = (40 \div 4) + (32 \div 4) \quad\quad = (60 \div 3) + (27 \div 3)$

$\quad\quad = 10 + 8 \quad\quad\quad\quad\quad\quad = 20 + 9$

$\quad\quad = 18 \quad\quad\quad\quad\quad\quad\quad = 29$

Copy and complete.

a $96 \div 3 = (90 + 6) \div 3$
$\quad\quad = (90 \div 3) + (6 \div 3)$
$\quad\quad =$
$\quad\quad =$

b $65 \div 5 = (60 + 5) \div 5$
$\quad\quad = (60 \div 5) + (5 \div 5)$
$\quad\quad =$
$\quad\quad =$

c $76 \div 4 = (40 + 36) \div 4$
$\quad\quad = (40 \div 4) + (36 \div 4)$
$\quad\quad =$
$\quad\quad =$

d $90 \div 5 = (50 + 40) \div 5$
$\quad\quad = (50 \div 5) + (40 \div 5)$
$\quad\quad =$
$\quad\quad =$

e $96 \div 4 = (80 + 16) \div 4$
$\quad\quad = (80 \div 4) + (16 \div 4)$
$\quad\quad =$
$\quad\quad =$

f $81 \div 3 = (60 + 21) \div 3$
$\quad\quad = (60 \div 3) + (21 \div 3)$
$\quad\quad =$
$\quad\quad =$

Copy and complete.

a $78 \div 3 =$ **b** $80 \div 5 =$ **c** $68 \div 4 =$

d $72 \div 6 =$ **e** $92 \div 4 =$ **f** $84 \div 6 =$

g $95 \div 5 =$ **h** $90 \div 6 =$ **i** $72 \div 3 =$

Copy and complete.

a $84 \div 3 =$ **b** $84 \div 7 =$ **c** $64 \div 4 =$

d $98 \div 7 =$ **e** $78 \div 6 =$ **f** $99 \div 9 =$

g $96 \div 6 =$ **h** $96 \div 8 =$ **i** $91 \div 7 =$

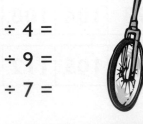

Puppy weights

 Know how many grams make 1 kilogram

Glenbrae Vets: clinic records

Parents: Dot and Dash

Puppies: Daisy, Dixie, Dolly

Puppy weights: 2 months

	kg	g
Daisy	5	500
Dixie	6	500
Dolly	4	500

Puppy weights: 4 months

	kg	g
Daisy	12	500
Dixie	12	0
Dolly	11	500

Puppy weights: 6 months

	kg	g
Daisy	16	800
Dixie	17	600
Dolly	16	500

Example

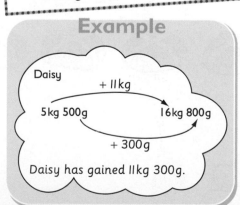

Daisy

+ 11 kg

5 kg 500 g   16 kg 800 g

+ 300 g

Daisy has gained 11 kg 300 g.

1 Copy and complete the weight for each puppy at 2 months.

Daisy weighs —— kg and —— g, or —— kg.

Dixie weighs —— kg and —— g, or —— kg.

Dolly weighs —— kg and —— g, or —— kg.

2 Copy and complete the weight for each puppy at 4 months.

Daisy weighs —— kg and —— g, or —— kg.

Dixie weighs —— kg and —— g, or —— kg.

Dolly weighs —— kg and —— g, or —— kg.

1 At 6 months, which puppy is

 a the heaviest?

 b 300 g lighter than Daisy?

 c 200 g less than 17 kg?

2 Look at the weights for 2 months and 6 months. Work out how much weight each puppy has gained.

 Work out how much weight each puppy has gained between 4 and 6 months.

Weighty problems

● **Make jottings and write calculations to answer a problem**

Write the better estimate of weight for each of these.

a a new-born baby

3 kg or 30 kg

b a mouse

30 g or 300 g

c a cat
30 g or 300 g
5 kg or 50 kg

d a dalmatian dog

25 kg or 250 kg

e a cow

70 kg or 700 kg

f an elephant
60 kg or 6000 kg

Solve these word problems. Show all your working.

a An egg weighs about 50 g.
About how much do 6 eggs weigh?

b The weight of a large loaf is 800 g.
How much will 3 loaves weigh?

c A box of 6 cheese triangles
weighs 180 g. Tom uses 3 triangles
of cheese for his sandwiches. What
weight of cheese is left in the box?

d A pack of 4 buns weighs 240 g.
What does 1 buns weigh?

A big potato weighs about 250 g.
What will be the weight of

a 4 big potatoes?

b 8 big potatoes?

c 10 big potatoes?

Wild West directions

● Use the four compass directions N, S, E, W to describe a direction

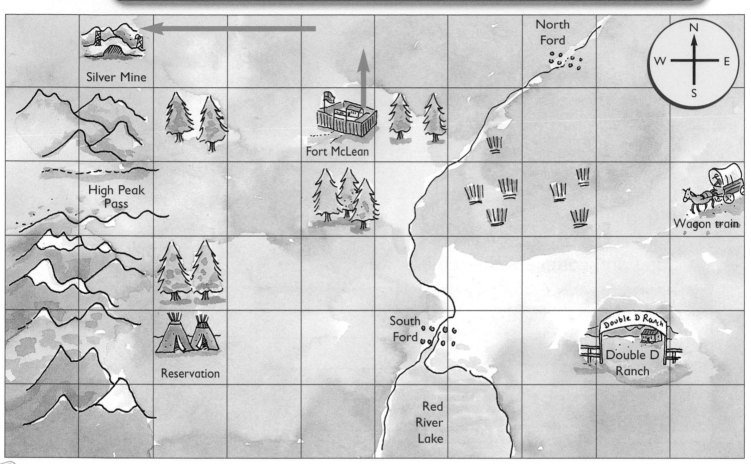

You are at Fort McLean. Where do these directions take you?

a 1 square north, 3 squares west.
b 1 square west, 1 square south, 2 squares west.
c 1 square west, 3 squares south, 1 square west.
d 1 square north, 4 squares east, 4 squares south.

Key:	
Dangerous	**Safe**
swamp	ford
forest	

You are with the wagon train. There are some dangers on the trail which you must avoid. You can only cross the Red River at a ford.

a Describe a safe route to Fort McLean.
b The wagon train is headed for the High Peak Pass in the mountains. Work out a safe route.
c Write a route to the Double D Ranch and then on to the Silver Mine.

The Indians on the Reservation want to reach North Ford. Write a route they might take to avoid detection by the cavalry at Fort McLean.

About turning

● **Follow and give instructions to make turns**

Copy and complete the table.

I face the	two $\frac{1}{4}$ turns right	I now face the
pyramid	→	
camel	→	
obelisk	→	
tour bus	→	

I turn two $\frac{1}{4}$ turns to my right…

Copy and complete the tables.

I face the	I make	I now face the
camel	two $\frac{1}{4}$ turns left	
obelisk	two $\frac{1}{4}$ turns right	
pyramid	a $\frac{1}{2}$ turn left	
tour bus	a $\frac{1}{2}$ turn right	

I face the	In the opposite direction	is the
pyramid	→	
obelisk	→	
camel	→	

Write what you see when you have made these moves.

a Face north. Make a $\frac{1}{2}$ turn left then a $\frac{1}{4}$ turn right.

b Face west. Make a $\frac{1}{4}$ turn left then a $\frac{1}{2}$ turn right.

c Face south. Make two $\frac{1}{4}$ turns right then a $\frac{1}{2}$ turn left.

Reflected patterns

● **Use shapes with right angles and reflective symmetry to make patterns**

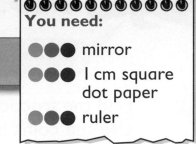
1 This triangle is reflected in a mirror.
Copy and continue the pattern on square dot paper as far as you can go. Check with your mirror.

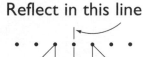
Reflect in this line

2 Copy and continue this pattern.

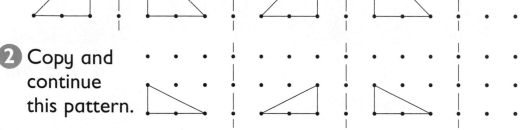

Continue each pattern on square dot paper by reflecting it in a mirror each time.
Mark the right angles.
Draw the mirror line.

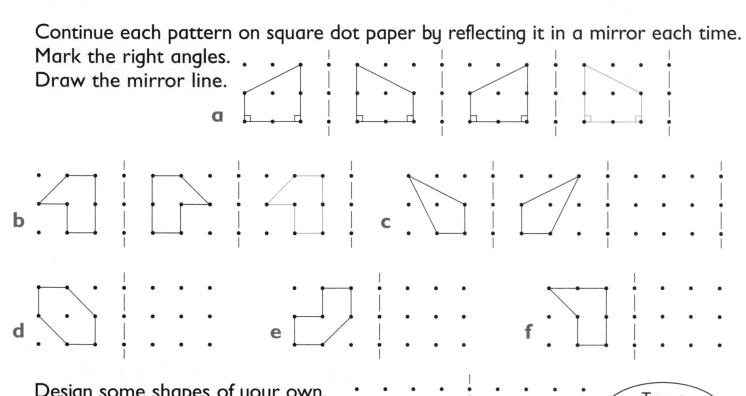

a
b
c
d
e
f

Design some shapes of your own.
Reflect them in the mirror line.
Describe how the pattern changes.

Try a 4 x 4 grid.

Money fractions

● **Find unit fractions of numbers and quantities**

Find the fractions of these amounts of money.
Use the coins in the purses to help you.

a $\frac{1}{2}$ of 30p   **b** $\frac{1}{2}$ of 70p   **c** $\frac{1}{5}$ of 50p   **d** $\frac{1}{4}$ of 20p

e $\frac{1}{4}$ of 60p   **f** $\frac{1}{3}$ of 30p   **g** $\frac{1}{3}$ of 18p

Find the fractions of these amounts of money. Write down the division
calculation that you used.

a $\frac{1}{2}$ of 14p   **b** $\frac{1}{2}$ of 90p   **c** $\frac{1}{4}$ of 48p

d $\frac{1}{4}$ of 80p   **e** $\frac{1}{3}$ of 12p   **f** $\frac{1}{3}$ of 60p

g $\frac{1}{5}$ of 25p   **h** $\frac{1}{5}$ of 50p   **i** $\frac{1}{10}$ of 90p

j $\frac{1}{10}$ of 70p   **k** $\frac{1}{4}$ of 60p   **l** $\frac{1}{5}$ of £1

❶ Explain why we use division to find fractions of amounts of money.
❷ Find $\frac{1}{2}$, $\frac{1}{4}$, and $\frac{1}{10}$ of £1.40. Show all your working.

Wall and window fractions

- **Identify fractions of shapes**

What fraction of the windows have been shaded over?

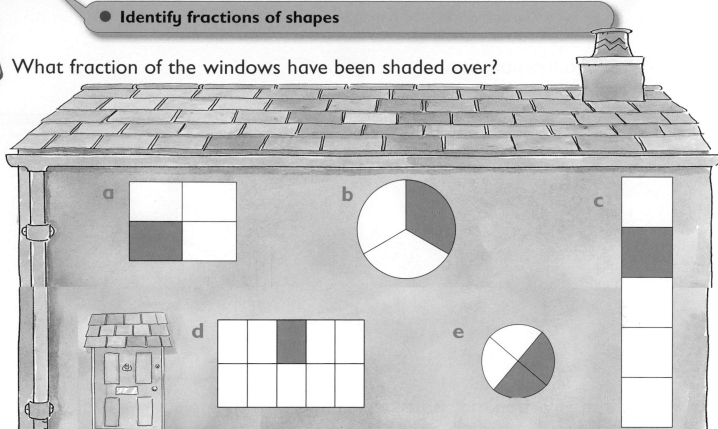

① What fraction of each wall is yellow?

a   b   c

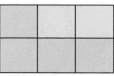  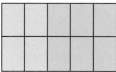

d   e   f

② What fraction of the wall has fallen down?

a   b   c   d   e

Draw some walls to match these fractions.

a $\frac{5}{6}$ b $\frac{3}{7}$ c $\frac{2}{8}$ d $\frac{4}{5}$ e $\frac{9}{10}$

Plate fractions

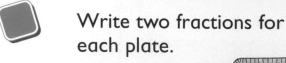
● **Identify and estimate fractions of shapes**

Write two fractions for each plate.

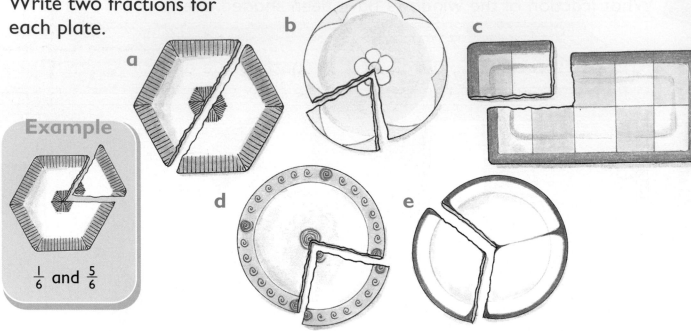

Example

$\frac{1}{6}$ and $\frac{5}{6}$

a

b

c

d

e

Write the fraction that is needed to make a whole plate.

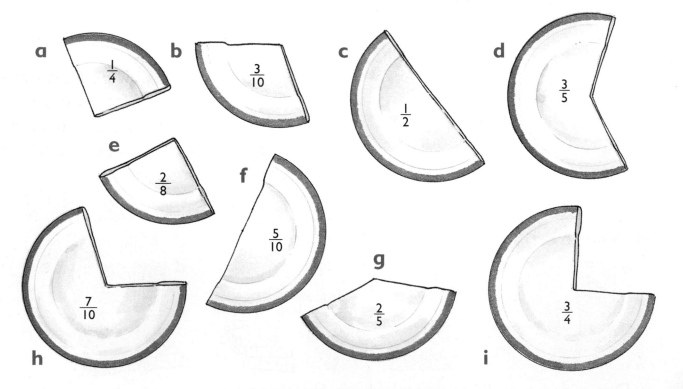

a $\frac{1}{4}$

b $\frac{3}{10}$

c $\frac{1}{2}$

d $\frac{3}{5}$

e $\frac{2}{8}$

f $\frac{5}{10}$

g $\frac{2}{5}$

h $\frac{7}{10}$

i $\frac{3}{4}$

Write two fractions that make half. How many different pairs can you think of?

Teatime halves and quarters

● Use diagrams to compare fractions and establish equivalents

You need:
● red, blue and yellow coloured pencils

1 Copy each cake. Colour half red, a quarter blue and a quarter yellow. Write $\frac{1}{2}$ or $\frac{1}{4}$ on the correct sections.

a   b   c   d

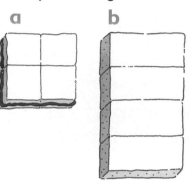

Example

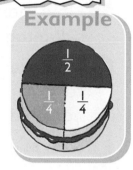

2 Ben gets half the biscuits. Amir and Emma get a quarter each. How many does each child get?

1 Join the halves and quarters to make whole cakes. Write down the letters that make a whole cake.

Then write the fractions that make each whole cake.

2 Gurjit gets half the biscuits. Zoe and Ann get a quarter each. How many does each child get?

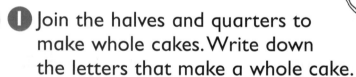

 Draw a cake made of a half and eighths.

Cake tray problems

● **Solve one-step and two-step word problems**

Mr Baker has made 12 currant buns and 8 jam tarts.

1 How many cakes does Mr Baker have to sell altogether?

2 Mr Baker arranges all the currant buns on to four plates. How many buns are on each plate?

3 Sam buys 5 jam tarts. How many are left?

4 Emma buys six currant buns for her and her sister to share. How many do they have each?

5 Tomorrow Mr Baker will bake double the number of buns and tarts. How many will he bake altogether?

William, Tim and Amy bought sweets for three weeks. William has 18, Tim has 9 more than William and Amy has twice as many as William.

1 How many sweets do William and Tim have altogether?

2 Every week William bought the same number of sweets. How many did he buy each week?

3 If they shared all their sweets equally, how many would they each get?

4 How many more sweets do William and Tim need each to have the same number as Amy?

Sweets are sold in bags of 6 for 24p and bags of 8 for 30p. Which is the cheapest way to buy them? How do you know?

Reviewing multiplication and division facts (2)

● **Know multiplication facts for the 2, 3, 4, 5, 6 and 10 times tables and the related division facts**

1 Copy and complete the following multiplication calculations.

a 8 × 3 = ☐   b 8 × 10 = ☐   c 10 × 4 = ☐   d 3 × 7 = ☐

e 4 × 8 = ☐   f 7 × 4 = ☐   g 5 × 5 = ☐   h 4 × 2 = ☐

i 9 × 3 = ☐   j 4 × 3 = ☐   k 9 × 6 = ☐   l 2 × 8 = ☐

m 5 × 7 = ☐   n 8 × 6 = ☐   o 5 × 10 = ☐   p 8 × 5 = ☐

2 Copy and complete the following division calculations.

a 36 ÷ 6 = ☐   b 20 ÷ 2 = ☐   c 16 ÷ 4 = ☐   d 24 ÷ 6 = ☐

e 8 ÷ 4 = ☐   f 42 ÷ 6 = ☐   g 12 ÷ 2 = ☐   h 25 ÷ 5 = ☐

i 16 ÷ 2 = ☐   j 15 ÷ 3 = ☐   k 45 ÷ 5 = ☐   l 24 ÷ 3 = ☐

m 12 ÷ 3 = ☐   n 30 ÷ 10 = ☐   o 70 ÷ 10 = ☐   p 35 ÷ 5 = ☐

Use the colour code for each of the digits 1–10 to answer the following calculations.

1	2	3	4	5	6	7	8	9	10

a × = ?   b × = ?   c × = ?

d × = ?   e × = ?   f ×  = ?

g × = ?   h × = ?   i  ×  = ?

j 35 ÷ = ?   k 12 ÷ = ?   l 20 ÷ = ?

m 36 ÷ 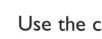 = ?   n 36 ÷ ? =    o 28 ÷ ? = ■

Use each set of three numbers to write 2 multiplication facts and 2 division facts.

a 4   28   7   b 27   3   9   c 18   3   6

d 4   8   32   e 8   40   5   f 7   6   42

Reviewing multiplication and division facts (3)

● Know multiplication facts for the 2, 3, 4, 5, 6 and 10 times tables and the related division facts

● Roll the two dice and use the two numbers to make a multiplication calculation.

● Multiply the two numbers together and write down the answer.

● Do this 10 times.

● Take turns to roll the dice, e.g. 4. If you roll a 1, roll the dice again.

● The person whose turn it is, places one of their counters on a multiple of the number rolled, i.e. 4, 8, 12, 16… and says the corresponding calculation, e.g. *12 divided by 4 equals 3.*

● If they cannot do this, they miss a turn.

● The winner is the first person to complete a column, row or diagonal of 4 numbers.

● The answer to the calculation, i.e. 3, is their score for that round. Keep a running total. Play 10 rounds. The winner is the person with the greater total.

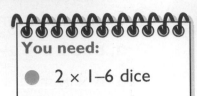

You need:
● 2 × 1–6 dice

You need:
●● 1–6 dice
●● 40 counters (20 of one colour, 20 of another colour)
● pencil
● paper

10	3	24	4	32	12
18	14	28	20	5	36
24	2	50	42	9	6
6	25	60	16	30	21
15	20	8	36	45	54
12	40	27	48	18	35

Doubles and halves

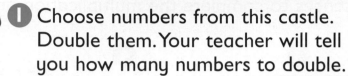
● Double whole numbers, multiples of 5 and
multiples of 10 and know the related halves

1 Choose numbers from this castle. Double them. Your teacher will tell you how many numbers to double.

2 Choose numbers from this castle. Halve them. Your teacher will tell you how many numbers to halve.

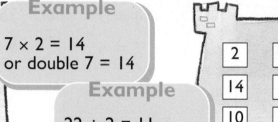

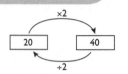

Example

$7 \times 2 = 14$
or double 7 = 14

Example

$22 \div 2 = 11$
or half of 22 = 11

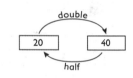

We can show that halving is the inverse (or opposite) of doubling by using a diagram like this.

Copy and fill in the missing numbers or operations on the diagrams.

a ×2 40 → ? ÷2

b ? 50 → ? ÷2

c double 25 → ? half

d ? ? → 70 half

e double 10 → ? ?

f ? ? → 90 ÷2

g ? ? → 30 ÷2

h ×? ? → 60 ?

i ? 35 → ? ?

Work with a partner.
Investigate

● Make 'doubles' using the number cards.
● Investigate different doubles that can be made using the cards.

You need:
● set of 0–9 digit cards

63

Multiplication versus division

 Know that division is the opposite of multiplication and vice versa

 Write the two missing number sentences to complete the multiplication and division number families.

1

$3 \times 6 = 18$
$6 \times 3 = 18$

2

$28 \div 4 = 7$
$28 \div 7 = 4$

3

$35 \div 7 = 5$
$5 \times 7 = 35$

4

$3 \times 8 = 24$
$24 \div 3 = 8$

 Some of these calculations are wrong. Copy the calculations. Draw a tick (✔) beside the answers that are right and a cross (✘) beside those that are wrong. For each wrong answer, write down the right answer.

Example

$24 \div 4 = 7$ ✘
$24 \div 4 = 6$

Name: Leo

1. $3 \times 6 = 18$
2. $4 \times 6 = 26$
3. $6 \times 9 = 52$
4. $10 \times 9 = 90$
5. $5 \times 7 = 35$
6. $8 \times 6 = 46$
7. $9 \times 2 = 27$
8. $5 \times 5 = 25$
9. $8 \times 4 = 34$
10. $9 \times 4 = 32$

Name: Rav

1. $42 \div 6 = 6$
2. $16 \div 4 = 3$
3. $16 \div 2 = 8$
4. $35 \div 5 = 6$
5. $18 \div 3 = 7$
6. $30 \div 3 = 10$
7. $10 \div 5 = 2$
8. $14 \div 2 = 9$
9. $12 \div 3 = 4$
10. $24 \div 3 = 7$

 ● Write a multiplication fact for the 4 times table. Then write the other related multiplication fact and the two related division facts.

Now...

● write a multiplication fact for the 3 and 10 times tables and write the other three related facts;

● write a division fact relating to the 5 and 6 times tables and write the other three related facts.

More fruit problems

● **Solve word problems involving 'real life' and money**

Read each word problem. Show all your working.

Apples
3 for 60p

Pears
5 for 50p

Strawberries
10 for 80p

Lemons
2 for 24p

Bunches of
grapes
4 for 80p

a How much for 1 strawberry?

b How much for 1 apple? How much for 2 apples?

c How much for 1 bunch of grapes?

d How much for 4 lemons?

e How much for 1 pear? How much for 2 pears?

If 10
strawberries cost
80p then 1 strawberry
must cost ...
80 ÷ 10 = ?

35 oranges

Read each word problem. Show all your working.

45 apples

80 bunches
of grapes

c The children take the same number of oranges to school each day. If the box is empty after five days, how many oranges were taken each day?

a A family eats 5 apples each day. How many days will one box last?

b The grocer sells ten bunches of grapes each day. How many days until the box is empty?

Strawberries
5 for 50p

Tomatoes
8 for 40p

Bananas
5 for 35p

d How much for ten strawberries?

e How much for eight strawberries?

f How much for two tomatoes?

g How much for six tomatoes?

h How much for three bananas?

i How much for ten bananas?

Using the information on this page about fruit, write three word problems for a friend to solve.

Starry doubles

● **Use doubling or halving, starting from known facts**

Double the number on each star and then double it again.

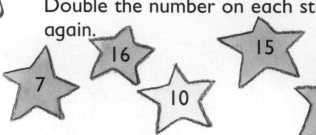

16   15   30   12

7   10   8   18   25   9

Example

6 + 6 = 12

12 + 12 = 24

Complete each 2 times table fact. Then open the card to find a 4 times table fact. Double your first answers to complete the facts for the 4 times table.

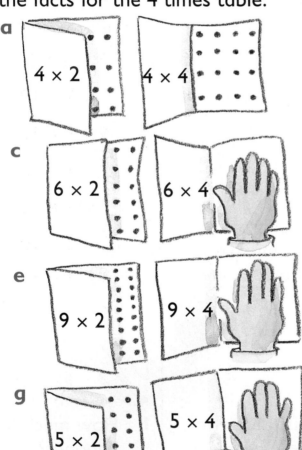

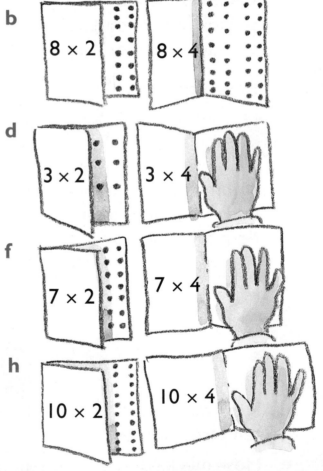

a 4 × 2   4 × 4

b 8 × 2   8 × 4

c 6 × 2   6 × 4

d 3 × 2   3 × 4

e 9 × 2   9 × 4

f 7 × 2   7 × 4

g 5 × 2   5 × 4

h 10 × 2   10 × 4

❶ Write some 3 times table facts and show how you can use these to work out the answers to the 6 times table.

❷ How are the 4 times table facts and 8 times table facts related? Give some examples to illustrate your explanation.

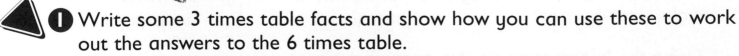

Multiplying multiples of 10

● **Multiply a multiple of 10 by a one-digit number**

Something has gone wrong with the computer. Find the calculations that are incorrect and rewrite them.

Copy each table. Write the answers.

a

× 2	
70	140
30	
40	
50	
60	

b

× 5	
30	
40	
90	
50	
20	

c

× 3	
50	
70	
40	
30	
20	

d

× 4	
40	
30	
80	
20	
50	

e

× 10	
70	
40	
20	
50	
30	

f

× 1	
40	
20	
30	
60	
50	

3 × 3 = 6

2 × 4 = 8

5 × 3 = 8

4 × 3 = 7

6 × 5 = 40

3 × 2 = 5

5 × 2 = 10

4 × 5 = 19

3 × 4 = 15

5 × 5 = 20

2 × 5 = 10

4 × 3 = 12

Use your multiplication facts to work out the missing number.

a 70 × ◯ = 280

b ◯ × 50 = 400

c ◯ × 6 = 540

d 6 × ◯ = 240

e ◯ × 4 = 120

f ◯ × 30 = 210

g ◯ × 90 = 270

h ◯ × 8 = 480

i 20 × ◯ = 180

Multiplying multiples of 10 and 100

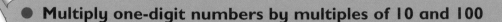

● **Multiply one-digit numbers by multiples of 10 and 100**

Copy and complete.

a 9 × 5 = ◯   b 8 × 2 = ◯   c 4 × 6 = ◯
d 4 × 9 = ◯   e 8 × 3 = ◯   f 4 × 3 = ◯
g 6 × 6 = ◯   h 4 × 4 = ◯   i 8 × 6 = ◯
j 5 × 8 = ◯   k 9 × 4 = ◯   l 9 × 2 = ◯
m 3 × 9 = ◯   n 7 × 6 = ◯   o 6 × 3 = ◯

1 Copy and complete each set of calculations.

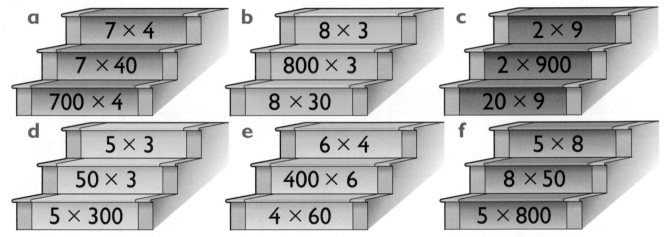

a 7 × 4 / 7 × 40 / 700 × 4
b 8 × 3 / 800 × 3 / 8 × 30
c 2 × 9 / 2 × 900 / 20 × 9
d 5 × 3 / 50 × 3 / 5 × 300
e 6 × 4 / 400 × 6 / 4 × 60
f 5 × 8 / 8 × 50 / 5 × 800

2 Use your knowledge of the times tables facts to help you work out the answers to these calculations.

a 700 × 3 = ◯   b 20 × 8 = ◯   c 5 × 70 = ◯
d 3 × 600 = ◯   e 80 × 3 = ◯   f 7 × 400 = ◯
g 8 × 30 = ◯   h 2 × 400 = ◯   i 3 × 90 = ◯
j 90 × 4 = ◯   k 500 × 2 = ◯   l 60 × 9 = ◯

Copy and complete.

a 400 × ◯ = 2000   b 8 × ◯ = 1600   c ◯ × 6 = 7200
d ◯ × 3 = 150   e 20 × ◯ = 180   f ◯ × 300 = 1800
g 4 × ◯ = 280   h 70 × ◯ = 420   i ◯ × 9 = 270
j 90 × ◯ = 180   k ◯ × 8 = 320   l ◯ × 700 = 2100

Finding remainders

● Divide a two-digit number by a one-digit number

 1 Copy and complete.

a 2 x 5   = ☐   b 3 x 10 = ☐

c 7 x 2   = ☐   d 3 x 3   = ☐

e 9 x 3   = ☐   f 20 ÷ 2 = ☐

g 30 ÷ 5 = ☐   h 50 ÷ 10 = ☐

i 15 ÷ 3 = ☐   j 12 ÷ 4 = ☐

2 There were 23 apples.
Sean put them into five bags of 4.
How many are left?

 Look at the number on
the yellow cube. Then
look at each number in
the coloured box and
write down the multiple
that is closest to, but not
over each number. Two
have been done for you.

5

16 →	15
12 →	☐
27 →	☐
33 →	☐
41 →	☐
52 →	50
36 →	☐
19 →	☐
29 →	☐
37 →	☐

10

43 →	☐
27 →	☐
62 →	☐
45 →	☐
51 →	☐
16 →	☐
24 →	☐
35 →	☐
96 →	☐
82 →	☐

4

13 →	☐
9 →	☐
23 →	☐
42 →	☐
37 →	☐
34 →	☐
6 →	☐
17 →	☐
21 →	☐
43 →	☐

 For each of the
sets of numbers in
the ⬤ section
above, write down
the division fact
including how
many are left over
(the remainder).

Example

16 ÷ 5 = 3 R 1
52 ÷ 5 = 10 R 2

Rounding remainders

● **Divide a two-digit number by a one-digit number**

Find the answer
to these division
calculations.
Be careful, some
have remainders.

a 25 ÷ 5 = ☐   b 11 ÷ 2 = ☐   c 30 ÷ 5 = ☐
d 30 ÷ 10 = ☐   e 22 ÷ 5 = ☐   f 22 ÷ 3 = ☐
g 16 ÷ 4 = ☐   h 43 ÷ 10 = ☐   i 76 ÷ 10 = ☐
j 12 ÷ 3 = ☐   k 16 ÷ 5 = ☐   l 43 ÷ 4 = ☐
m 20 ÷ 2 = ☐   n 10 ÷ 3 = ☐   o 17 ÷ 2 = ☐

Read each word problem. Write the division fact and
the answer. If there is a remainder, think carefully
whether you need to round your answer up or down.

Remember
to show your
working.

a There are 16 children.
Five children can fit in
a car. How many cars
do you need?

b Tickets for the
waterslide cost £5 each. I
have £46. How many
tickets can I buy?

c I have 38 cakes.
One box holds five
cakes. How many
boxes do I need to
hold all my cakes?

d There are 27 children.
A table seats four.
How many tables are
needed to seat all the
children?

e Packets of balloons cost £3. I have
£16. How many packets of
balloons can I buy?

f I have 46 sweets to give to four
children. How many sweets do they
get each if they all receive an equal
share?

For each of the following calculations write two word problems. One where
you need to round the answer up and the other where you need to round
the answer down. ↑ 27 ÷ 4 ↓   ↑ 45 ÷ 6 ↓

Maths Facts

Problem solving

The seven steps to problem solving

❶ Read the problem carefully. ❷ What do you have to find?

❸ What facts are given? ❹ Which of the facts do you need?

❺ Make a plan. ❻ Carry out your plan to obtain your answer. ❼ Check your answer.

Number

Positive and negative numbers

Place value

1000	2000	3000	4000	5000	6000	7000	8000	9000
100	200	300	400	500	600	700	800	900
10	20	30	40	50	60	70	80	90
1	2	3	4	5	6	7	8	9

Number facts

Multiplication and division facts

	×1	×2	×3	×4	×5	×6	×7	×8	×9	×10
×1	1	2	3	4	5	6	7	8	9	10
×2	2	4	6	8	10	12	14	16	18	20
×3	3	6	9	12	15	18	21	24	27	30
×4	4	8	12	16	20	24	28	32	36	40
×5	5	10	15	20	25	30	35	40	45	50
×6	6	12	18	24	30	36	42	48	54	60
×7	7	14	21	28	35	42	49	56	63	70
×8	8	16	24	32	40	48	56	64	72	80
×9	9	18	27	36	45	54	63	72	81	90
×10	10	20	30	40	50	60	70	80	90	100

Fractions and decimals

$\frac{1}{2}$ $\frac{1}{4}$ $\frac{1}{8}$ $\frac{1}{3}$ $\frac{1}{6}$ $\frac{1}{9}$ $\frac{1}{12}$ $\frac{1}{5}$ $\frac{1}{10}$

Calculations

Addition

Whole numbers
Example: 845 + 758

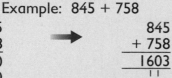

```
  845              845
+ 758            + 758
 1500             1603
   90               ¹¹
   13
 1603
   ¹
```

Money
Example: £26.48 + £53.75

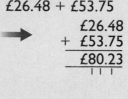

```
 £26.48           £26.48
+£53.75          +£53.75
  70.00           £80.23
   9.00             ¹ ¹ ¹
   1.10
   0.13
 £80.23
    ¹
```

Calculations

Subtraction

Example: 162 − 115

```
  162              162                              50  12                   5 12
−   5            − 115                 100 + 6̶0 + 2̶                    1̶6̶2̶
────             ────                 − 100 + 10 + 5                  − 115
  157                5 → 120          ─────────────                  ─────
−  10               42 → 162              40 + 7                        47
────             ────
  147               47
− 100
────
   47
```

Multiplication

Example: 82 × 7

Grid method   or   Partitioning

$82 \times 7 = (80 \times 7) + (2 \times 7)$

$= 560 + 14$

$= 574$

×	80	2
7	560	14	= 574

```
      82
    ×  7
    ───
    560   (80 × 7)
     14   ( 2 × 7)
    ───
    574
```
→
```
      82
    ×  7
    ───
    560
     14
    ───
    574
```
→
```
      82
    ×  7
    ───
    574
     ₁
```

Division

Example: 87 ÷ 5

$87 \div 5 = (50 + 37) \div 5$

$= (50 \div 5) + (37 \div 5)$

$= 10 + 7 \ R \ 2$

$= 17 \ R \ 2$

or

```
      87
   −  50   (10 × 5)
   ────
      37
   −  35   ( 7 × 5)
   ────
       2
```

Answer   17 R 2

or

```
5)   87
   − 50   (10 × 5)
   ────
     37
   − 35   ( 7 × 5)
   ────
      2
```

Answer   17 R 2

Shape and space

2–D shapes

    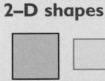    

circle   right-angled triangle   equilateral triangle   isosceles triangle   square   rectangle   pentagon   hexagon   heptagon   octagon

3–D shapes

cube   cuboid   cone   cylinder   sphere   triangular prism   triangular-based pyramid (tetrahedron)   square-based pyramid